Same
Old
Story

Dawn Potter

Same
Old
Story

CavanKerry ❖ Press LTD.

CavanKerry Press Ltd.
Fort Lee, New Jersey
www.cavankerrypress.org

Library of Congress Cataloging-in-Publication Data

Potter, Dawn, 1964-
[Poems. Selections]
Same old story / Dawn Potter. -- First Edition.
pages cm.
Poems.
ISBN 978-1-933880-40-2 (alk. paper) -- ISBN 1-933880-40-6 (alk. paper)
I. Title.

PS3616.O8485A6 2014
811'.6--dc23

2013021341

Cover photograph by Thomas Birtwistle © 2012
Cover and interior text design by Gregory Smith

First Edition 2014, Printed in the United States of America

NOTABLE VOICES
CavanKerry ❧ Press

CavanKerry Press is proud to publish the works
of established poets of merit and distinction.

Discover
JERSEY
ARTS

NEW JERSEY
STATE COUNCIL
ON THE ARTS

CavanKerry Press is grateful for the support it receives
from the New Jersey State Council on the Arts.

Other Books by Dawn Potter

POETRY

Boy Land & Other Poems (2004)
How the Crimes Happened (2010)

PROSE

Tracing Paradise: Two Years in Harmony with John Milton (2009)
The Vagabond's Bookshelf (2014)
The Conversation: Learning to Be a Poet (2014)

ANTHOLOGY

*A Poet's Sourcebook: Writings about Poetry,
from the Ancient World to the Present* (2013)

for Tom

Why is my verse so barren of new pride?
So far from variation or quick change?
Why with time do I not glance aside
To new-found methods and to compounds strange?
Why write I still all one, ever the same,
And keep invention in a noted weed,
That every word doth almost tell my name,
Showing their birth, and where they did proceed?
O, know, sweet love, I always write of you,
And you and love are still my argument;
So all my best is dressing old words new,
Spending again what is already spent:
      For as the sun is daily new and old,
      So is my love still telling what is told.

William Shakespeare, sonnet 76

Contents

Contents

III

IV

V

Prologue

Driving Lesson

Neither son nor father slept that night.
Tangled in sheets, the wide-eyed boy
stared into the chamber's pearly dark.
He twitched his hands on the pillows,
guiding the heads of invisible horses.
From the apex of heaven, he saluted
his awestruck mother as her neighbors
sank to their knees in tardy admiration.

His father made no pretense of dreaming.
Late into the night, he sat in his throne room
watching the stars wander the heavens—
braggart Orion cinching his belt, the clumsy Bull
pawing at a black meadow. But toward morning,
before Dawn could arise from her bed in the east,
the god was in the stable, running practiced hands
over wheels and axle, checking hooves for stones.

When Phaeton appeared, crumpled and shining,

the Sun was leading his winged horses from their stalls.

Rested, well-fed, they tugged against their halters,

and at each breath, fire flared from their nostrils.

Through the stable gate, the god and his son glimpsed

Dawn unfolding her rosy sash on the horizon.

The Moon's curl had vanished, and far below the palace,

Earth's blue outline trembled under coils of mist.

As the Sun harnessed the stamping horses,

backing them four abreast, snorting and dancing,

into the chariot's jeweled yoke, he advised Phaeton

on how best to manage the unruly team.

Though his voice was steady, his gestures calm,

his heart was heavy with foreboding.

After each caution, the boy nodded.

His eyes glowed. Perhaps he was listening.

"Leave the whip alone," said the god.

"Keep your weight on the reins.

Holding back is your hardest task.

Earth and sky need equal magnitudes of heat.

Follow the middle road; my wheel tracks are clear.

And there is still time, plenty of time, to change your mind.

Give me the reins; go, eat something,

and we will sit together under the Moon tonight."

But the boy had already climbed into the chariot.
There he stood, tense as a hare, clutching the reins —
joyful, oblivious, smiling up at his father.
Where was the terror that yesterday
had burdened him like a barrow of slag?
The horses snorted, snapped their gilded wings,
rang their hooves against the bronze bars of the gate.
The chariot trembled on its gleaming wheels.

Leaning into the car, the Sun kissed his child.
Then he lifted the fiery crown from his head,
tightened it, and slipped it over Phaeton's curls.
"You see, it doesn't burn me!" cried the boy,
proudly tossing his cumbered hair. "Father,
watch me at noon! Watch me wave to you!"
But the time for talk was gone. Dawn's gaudy robe
blanketed the sky, and the Sun heaved open the gate.

Same
Old
Story

I

It is sometimes curiously difficult to name
the emotion from which one suffers.

—Iris Murdoch, *The Black Prince*

Astrolabe

Like a flour smudge on an old blue apron,
A lunchtime moon thumbprints the sun-plowed,
Snow-scrabbled heavens of Harmony, Maine.
Last night three cops shot Danny McDowell
On South Road, down by the shack you and I rented
That hard winter when the northern lights glowed
And the washing machine froze and I got pregnant.
I built a five-inch snowboy for our half-inch embryo.
You took a picture of it cradled in my mittens.
But today, too late, too late, I see I forgot to worry
About this moon, this ominous rock waxing half-bitten
Over our clueless sentimental history.
        Picture it falling. A white egg, neat and slow.
        It doubles. Redoubles. Till all we see is shadow.

Ugly Town

The sun is under no obligation to shed its optimistic beams
        on the ugliest town in Maine—not now, not in March
when I've steeled myself for gravel-picked mud and despair,
        for broken branches and a plow-scarred dooryard
rimmed with a winter's worth of dog turds, pale and crumbled
        among the pale remaindered weeds.

But it does shine, that fool's orb, for reasons best known to itself;
        and I slouch here in my yellow chair, both cold feet
parked under the woodstove, squinting into this cheerful, bossy glare,
        attempting to convince myself that unbridled nature
has, for once, chosen to be a genial master instead of the flogging brute
        we expect here in the ugly town, where we don't think

ski but *shovel*, don't think *flowers* but *floods*.
        Maybe I've been reading too many books—
too much Roth and Munro, too much Blake and Carruth,
        all of them driven to detail bleak empty roads
and unmown lawns; evil alleys and poisonous rivers;
        the fathers, dyspeptic, misunderstood; the mothers,

wiping schmaltz and ketchup from the shabby oilcloth; and meanwhile
        those thirteen angels on their magic seats, frowning and perturbed.
Of course there's happiness too. No one denies the happiness,
        but don't count on it to carry you through. Keep your eye
steady, your irony sharp. Stay wary; it's best to stay wary—
        though not one of these writers, I can tell you right now,

has ever stayed wary enough, and they've paid for it in spades —
  a phrase that might, for dwellers of another clime,
connote cognac and midnight whist parties
  but that here, in the ugly town, where most everyone
gambles by scratch ticket and goes to bed early,
  means plain old digging:

in snow, in thankless stony soil, with a bent shovel,
  with a belching backhoe; tearing up asphalt,
forking out a winter's worth of choking black shit.
  You can kill yourself when you pay in spades
for a neat square cellar hole — say, when you're fifty years married
  to a woman who's dreamed for all those heavy decades

of trading her wind-licked trailer for a house with a furnace.
  No, you haven't had time, you haven't had money,
all you've had is a middle-aged kid who won't get out of the recliner
  except to grab a beer from the icebox, all you've had
are those cars, one after the other, falling into seizures and dismay;
  and if you can't stop eating what you shouldn't be eating,

at least there's salt, there's sugar, those reliable offerings
  that remind you you're still alive, that you haven't yet
paid out every single spade. Yet it's a lie, and you know it,
  and I know it too because I tell my own brand of lies,
such as *it's okay to be easy on myself,*
  such as *I mean well,* such as *it's good enough*

to chronicle the sweetness of this sunlight,
  not to force myself to keep struggling to speak

when I don't know how to think, when I don't know how
        to find the word, the only word, trembling, naked as a rat,
when I don't know how to lay it down, wet and mewling,
        among the schmaltz and the ketchup stains.

Someone might argue that here's where a little wariness
        would do me good, and not just me but all these writers
whose books I've been reading too often,
        and even they might agree with you, on a bad morning.
But today, according to this obstinate sun, is not a bad morning.
        Brilliance leaks and flows through window smears,

patches the dour carpet. The light refuses to let up.
        It insists on itself, like a mean cat does,
gliding from nowhere to bite me on the ankle.
        The world is too much with us; late and soon
is what Wordsworth wrote, but it's not what he meant.
        He was trying to say we were too distracted by our lives

to notice this sunshine, and here I am borrowing his words
        to explain that I am too distracted by this sunshine
to notice my life. The world overtakes me,
        I'm not wary enough, and something bad *will* happen
if I don't watch out. That's the point to remember about writing.
        It doesn't solve anything.

Home

So wild it was when we first settled here.
Spruce roots invaded the cellar like thieves.
Skunks bred on the doorstep, cluster flies jeered.
Ice-melt dripped shingles and screws from the eaves.
We slept by the stove, we ate meals with our hands.
At dusk we heard gunshots, and wind and guitars.
We imagined a house with a faucet that ran
From a well that held water. We canvassed the stars.
If love is an island, what map was our hovel?
Dogs howled on the mainland, our cliff washed away.
We hunted for clues with a broken-backed shovel.
We drank all the wine, night dwindled to grey.
        When we left, a flat sunrise was threatening snow,
        But the frost heaves were deep. We had to drive slow.

Spring on the Ripley Road

Knick knack, paddywhack,
Ordering the sun,
Learning planets sure is fun.

—Paul's backseat song

Five o'clock, first week of daylight savings.
Sunshine doggedly pursues night.
Pencil-thin, the naked maples cling to winter.

James complains,
"It's *orbiting*, not *ordering*."

Everything is an argument.
The salt-scarred car rockets through potholes,
hurtles over frostbitten swells of asphalt.

James explains, "The planets orbit the sun.
Everything lives in the universe."

Sky blunders into trees.
A fox, back-lit, slips across the road
and vanishes into an ice-clogged culvert.

Paul shouts, "Even Jupiter? Even foxes?
Even grass? Even underwear?"

Trailers squat by rusted plow trucks;
horses bow their searching, heavy heads.
The car dips and spins over the angry tar.

James complains, "I'm giving you facts.
Why are you so annoying?"

The town rises from its petty valley.
Crows, jeering, sail into the pines,
and the river tears at the dam.

Paul shouts, "Dirt lives in the universe!
I *want* to be annoying!"

Everywhere, mud.
Last autumn's Marlboro packs,
faded and derelict, shimmer in the ditch.

James says,
"When you get an F in life
it'll be your own fault."

Blue in Green

Talk about art being its own worst
story: once I made the mistake
of playing *Kind of Blue* to snare
a baby into slumber.

Compare the crime
to those water-green lilies that teachers
Scotch-tape over the reading corner.
Now picture Monet shuffling the hallways
among our fluorescent children.
He would die of remorse. Meanwhile,
I knifed Miles for the sake of an hour's
enchanted sleep. Who knew how soon
that breathing baby would light out
screaming into the blue?

II

But half the sorrows of women would be averted if they could repress the speech they know to be useless; nay, the speech they have resolved not to utter.

—George Eliot, *Felix Holt, the Radical*

After Twenty Years

It is possible
that no husband really loves his wife.

Too easy it is to mistake
their scheduled arrivals and departures, their constancy,
for something greater than the dim outcroppings
of loneliness.

When, entrapped again
in the fervent throes of habit,
we cry, "Do you love me?"
they answer yes.

Their manners
are faultless, restrained.
They sleep deeply,
and, in the morning, scraping ashes from the stove,

only rarely do they forget to speak.

No Day Is Safe from News of You

Morning breaks like glass.
I sidle through the kitchen,
naked as a hoptoad, but nary a glance
hipes my way.
My love, he loves me with an H; he feeds me
with hay and hieroglyphs. *Hélas*.

Cold wind blusters under a second-rate sun.
The speckled rooster hoicks his brag to heaven.
Our only news is bad news,
squawk his twelve insatiable hens.
Their feathers blow backward. In the patchy daylight
they shimmer like a straggle of dahlias.

Sing ho for the new year, croons the magazine to an empty room.
The stovepipe ticks,
but *Nothing, nothing, nothing,* says the clock.
My love, he loves me with an H; we breakfast
on hum-birds and humble pie,
though yesterday we ate husks.

Time flies! shouts the rooster, and the yeast agrees.
It swims in a blue bowl,
morning-glory blue, color of a blind eye.
Every headlong day my love's heart sings,
Weariness, yes, weariness, and never enough cash.
O holy night-before-last, when it forgot the words,

when I dreamt of turrets and stairs. Only
the radio kept muttering the tune.

Son-in-Law

She's on her knees, leaning over the tub,
wringing the grimy wet from an old woolen sweater,
watching the blackened circles of water fold themselves

down, down into the battered bathtub drain
that leads to the cesspool, that leads to the sluggish river.
And just as the whirlpool's rattle slips into silence,

and her knees have begun to memorize the ridged floor
pressing its patterns and flourishes into her thinning skin,
the phone rings for the second time this morning.

"How you been?" he asks when she picks up,
and she answers, "Oh, not too bad,"
as if they hadn't solemnly bowed their way

through this dance two hours ago,
while she was emptying last year's freezer-wizened beans
into the chicken pail, while she was counting

cans of juice and packages of pork chops.
But if she's already told him about the old camper—
"The one back in the woods, back there

behind my cousin Dave's place. You know,
the body's a wreck but Ralph's figuring
to haul it out so he can salvage the motor,"

or about the dahlias she's planted —
"Red ones they should of been, and purple
with a little stripe, but every last one came up yellow" —

he won't care. This is what he wants, really:
stories that don't matter to anyone;
and relaying her harmless gossip,

she feels her voice deepen and stretch,
as if she's a cassette tape spooling out at half speed.
She listens to his eager perfunctory replies,

and her eyes prickle with the pity of it,
a pity that hurts her like her knees hurt
when they're remembering their pattern of sorrow.

"He's the children's father" is all she can think to say
to the neighbors who want her to stop picking up the phone.
She won't go so far as to remind them,

"Oh, don't he miss those kids," but that's the truth.
Why else would he have locked them in that room,
and waved that gun, and howled? Why else,

if he hadn't understood he'd lost the game,
hadn't marked himself as dead?
He's no surprise to her; so when he wails down the line,

"I won't never see them again!" all she says is
"I got your clean shirts folded here on the bar."
With a swagger he shouts back, "I ain't afraid of you!"

and still he's like the boy he used to be,
the one she recalls at summer Bible school,
pouring Kool-Aid on her little girl

because he couldn't stop needing the joy
of that freckled outrage.
Anger always did soothe him. It always did.

"I'll get up to, your place, one of these days,"
he stammers now, and "I know you will,"
she says, mild as rain, before she lets herself

hang up the phone, before she sits down
at the vinyl tablecloth and cries a little,
before she takes herself back to her own dirty work.

Shouting at Shakespeare

How can you make such outrageous modest claims—
"I think good thoughts whilst other write good words"?
Why invite pity from the copyist mouthing your refrains
Like an accurate parrot? Why burden me with this absurd
Maudlin plea? The problem, big Will, is that no one
Can possibly trust your coy ignorance—these self-slamming asides,
These parenthetical sighs. You toss me a melancholy bone,
A morsel to sustain me as I dutifully admire your rhymes
And indiscretions. It's too much like dealing with the man
Who broods so charmingly on why he'll always love
My husband. I clutch the phone to my ear and fan
A panicked SOS into the resigned aether. Enough.
        I've grown used to the common pain
        Of being less. But don't you complain.

Letter to Will

He is chainsawing
And has decided
To love me
Again, I think.
Last night he
Ran his hands
Through my hair,
Down the nape,
Of my neck,
Kissed me between
The shoulder blades,
And so on.
But I lay
On my side
In another world.
It was like
Having the flu,
Or wearing 3-D
Glasses. I was
Tired, not knowing
What he meant
By kissing me.
Maybe tonight he'll
Still be happy
Enough, almost talking
To me, eating
Sour apple tart,

Watching a French
Movie with his
Head in my
Lap. We stumble
On and on.

III

I know, of course, that she once had a half-baked affair with a poet—
but, Heaven deliver us, what's a poet? Something that can't go to bed
without making a song about it.

—Dorothy L. Sayers, *Busman's Honeymoon*

Dog in Winter

Up the boggy headland, frozen now, where a stone fence
Submerged in snow and earth-sink hints at pasture
So long vanished that the woods are convinced
Grassland never existed, two bodies climb—one fast,
Black, doe-agile; one slogging and foot-bound
Like a superannuated tortoise. Guess which is me.
Easy to badmouth my grace but oddly hard to expound
On the postcard beauties of our workaday scenery—
Giant pines draped with frosting, wisp of chimney cloud
Threading skyward, and behind the frosted window
A glorious wall of books, lamp-lit; a dear bowed head.
In tales, common enchantment always merits less than woe,
 And perhaps I should collapse on the stoop like a starved Jane Eyre,
 Pleading heat and mercy. But I earn my joy. I mean, I live here.

Blue

Once upon a time there is an hour,
        rainless, starless. And then
a subtle hand unmasks a claw.
        Bone speaks to bone. A cower
roughens a curve; famine gnaws
        at tender flanks, grips bone, again,
again, tearing, shredding, once upon a time
        sleep pretends to fight, once
an hour shivers into dead rain, dry stars;
        into glory, first maculate chime
of defeat—bruise or savor, a barred
        owl's wail, the shrew that it hunts.

Elegy for a One-Night Stand

What I remember about you
is that you were too good for me;
so it's easy to recall, these decades since,
that I never believed that you would love me —

you, with your rich-boy clothes,
and the way you knew exactly what you were up to
when you let your palm slip down the small of my back.
But I think I'm right in recollecting we were happy

for the hour or two we borrowed that night,
and I want to claim that it was raining
and that the streetlight outside our grimy window
filtered a shimmer edge along your shoulders,

that your fingers read the bones of my face
as if they really did long to imagine what I longed for.
Now, after twenty years spent forgetting
anything we'd once learned about the other,

I begin to summon up the urgency that lured us there,
to someone else's street-lit bed, a room,
you claim, that glowed a baby-aspirin pink,
a shade I can't recall, though I think

I may have memorized your shadow-tilted head,
cocked as if to warn me: don't believe a word he says.
Don't fret. I didn't.
You never broke my heart; I grant you that achievement,

not easy to accomplish with a china heart like mine,
so liable to be chipped. You tell me now,
you throw yourself too much into your men.
Well, yes.

But what's the point of love that doesn't shatter?
It's the vice I've clung to; I never do get over anyone—
even you, my not-heartbreaker,
with the softest lips I've ever kissed, and then

that quickened breath against my throat,
those tender hands,
as weighted and exact as birds, and how my eyes
forgot their blue and, startled, turned to yours.

Cover Song

Once I had a boyfriend (you'll laugh, I know)
Who strolling at midnight through a yellow-brick alley
Grasped both my cold hands and sweetly bellowed
"My Girl" into the small wind that ebbed and sallied
Between our shadows. I'd known him for a week.
He stared into my eyes and slowly decanted Motown
Into the chill particulate air. Ignoring us, a plane idly streaked
Toward Philly, a bus hooted, a few cars sifted by. I looked down
At our four trapped hands: bowled over, yes, though fighting
A queasy embarrassment. But you know, better than most,
What I mean: how unreal it feels to play at romance, gliding
Slickly beyond your homely self like a ballroom ghost,

      As if your everyday, tempted, shivering skin
      Couldn't perform a truer rendition.

Valentine's Day

The plow guy shows up four hours after the snow has stopped
and plows a rosebush.
But in the dark of the year
I don't care about roses.
What I care about is an emergency exit to the street
so I can escape from my own toils and devices,

a hatch that he carves out for me,
after a fashion,
though it's littered with cigarette butts
and speckles of hydraulic fluid.
When I trudge out to hand him his cash,
he doesn't even bother

to transfer the joint to the other hand.
He smiles broadly, like a man should smile
when he's just finished plowing the driveway
of a woman who's rumored to write poems,
who's ten years older than himself,
and whose son plays soccer on his daughter's team,

where they do real good
because both kids are fast and can score, and once
they even got their names drawn from plastic pickle jars
and had to dance together at the middle-school Snow Ball.
Not that they liked it.
I feel a little sad

when the plow guy doesn't go so far
as to offer me the joint.
It's a disappointment,
but, in the long run,
probably for the best
since, if we did smoke a joint together —

his plaid elbow poking out of the pickup window,
me with my bare feet stuck into barn boots
and the zipper half torn out of my coat —
we might have to talk about something
like ice fishing,
or how big our skinny kids are getting,

or what the cold's supposed to do tomorrow,
instead of just plowing and smiling, and paying,
and turning our backs
in the way citizens do
who've modestly eyed each other for a score of years
but won't believe they have a life in common,

except for snow
and old clothes, and two kids
who chase a ball down a shaggy field.
Though now we share this morning's dose of loneliness.
God forbid
that we should mention such a thing.

IV

'Tis strange that they should so depart from home,
And not send back my messenger.

—William Shakespeare, *King Lear*

Mrs. Dickinson Waits in the Car

My Mother does not care for thought

— Emily Dickinson

A few meager stars, a hazy moon
brighter than old Kentuck,
and a bulge of frost spooned
across the windshield like a plucked,

flash-frozen chick. Into this arctic
chariot, the heater chafes and spouts
its idiot vows. Yes, I lied about Kentuck.
No doubt, it's glowing like all get-out,

like a pair of gibbous moons, like molten
honey dripped into a summer lake.
Blame art, then: I've been soaking up Bolton's
poems, and now I'm acting like a fake

southerner, which is to say gothically
depressed while making love to every rum-
soaked predicate I meet. Treat *gothically*
as a ringer for New England numb.

Today a friendly rube lauded my skill
at prosy contemplation, but what a crock.
Call a heart a spade: call me a fading, moody kill-
joy with a romance eye for loss and schlock.

The car fan chatters hopelessly; newsmen
chant wind-chill rates and hockey stats.
Like any hausfrau I fret over loaves in the oven,
socks on the line, carboys of milk, and ruinous vats

of soup. There they burn or boil.
Here I dally in this wrapper-strewn capsule,
this (laugh with me!) bell jar. Can I stand loyal
to her, cruel queen of diction, and also rule

my roost, my squat piratical outpost?
I shiver; I prop my tome of poems
against the cruiser's plastic wheel. I boast
that they age for me: these jeroboams

of syntax, these sherry cups of rage.
Yet these tired hands; yet these cold feet.
Go ahead: remind me to shut up, to flip the page,
to change the station, to bleat

of Mother's lonely vigil.
I'm not proud of my idle arrogance.
Meanwhile, the rye loaf chars and the milk spills.
They're out of my ken, for a hatful of minutes.

Let me claim to be oracular.
"Poetry is not like reasoning," urges Shelley.
And I reply: "nothing in particular"
is the maiden speech of every tragedy.

Girls and Their Cats and Their Stories

was the title of a work I composed last night
beneath the sweetly chimerical blanket
known as dead-dog sleep.

Grammar mattered in this tale,
and *Not* was its first word.
The story was priming itself to inhabit
the white space around a silhouette.

Yet in my dream I also glimpsed a picture —
a portrait, perhaps, of *Not*.
What I saw was a door: dark, paint-streaked;
blue-black as a bruise but dense, as if the painter
had concealed the door's true color
beneath layer upon layer of evasion.

And after I dreamed this door,
I dreamed the second word.
The word was *the*.

Now the story was donning its allotted garments;
now grammar, in silks and velvet,
had paced its first long strides
down the broad and noble corridor.
For *the* is an article of faith
binding itself to weary flesh and ancient cities,
even to the ambiguities of hope —

for, yes, now *house* reaches out to clutch
the's small and eager hand.

A house, a door, a negative, an article of faith.
They tried to tell a story.
But the only other word, the final word, was *that*.

No dash, no question mark
no busybody verb or self-indulgent pronoun.
Neither *cat* nor *girl*.
No person from Porlock to blame, as Coleridge did;
not even "and then I woke and learned it was a dream."

Merely, there was no sentence.

❀

Donna's story:
"When I was a girl I had cats.
In our kind of family my cat was all I had.
Knowing that she was going to purr in my ear
as I fell asleep was a comfort and I felt like
at least something might love me."

Dawn's story:
"My mother and I invented long
elaborate tales about a cat whose mother
lived on Pointy Head Street and belonged
to an evangelical congregation called
the Church of the Trap Door."

Dawn's other story:
"Not the house that
I dreamed of: where I ran up and up
the endless stairs clutching the cat
to my chest so the cat skinners wouldn't kill it
and then the cat began wailing howling yowling."

❊

When is a dream not a dream
   but the sentence I never wrote?
     When is the person from Porlock
       the cat scratching at the door? When
        is the door the trapdoor, the cat
         the cat killer, the sentence
          the dream?

❊

"Girls and Their Cats and Their Stories"
was the name of the work I meant to write

before I was interrupted by the person from Porlock
disguised as a fragment of *Not*.

As Auden remarks, Coleridge should have tried harder
to finish "Kubla Khan." As Auden might have remarked,

cats are a sentimental trap, and here Coleridge interrupts
to mention that he himself admires cats from Porlock

though he usually neglects to feed them.
The Khan remains silent.

No one in this poem forgets
that he slices off the heads of cats for sport.

＊

The person from Porlock's story:
    "'Girls and Their Cats and Their Stories'
    was the title of the final poem she wrote
    before she fell silent. And I'll be honest with you:
nobody likes this piece. It's an irritant,
    a flake of grit in the eye of the tiny public
    that adored those cheerful verses
    about children and Keats and country hi-jinks
that she cranked out so reliably
    and published to such moderate acclaim.
    This poem . . . I'll be honest:
    it's a mess, as if she wasted too much time
poring over literary magazines
    while running a high fever.
    A shame, I'd say,
    that this is what we're stuck with—
a few maundering flippancies;
    a hand with a flashlight groping in the dark,
    mistaking the cat
    for the bathroom switch."

＊

(Meanwhile, the door remained shut.
The glow of a streetlight picked out the runnels of paint —
blue-black, scratched here and there as if someone
had picked at it with the tines of a fork.
Under the streetlight, the paint
clung to the door like mud.
A smell of cat rose from the gutters;
and now the rain, which had threatened all day,
began to fall, the first slow drops striking
the low roofs, the blank-faced walls, a slop-
shouldered girl who was singing to herself
as she shoved a lame shopping cart
up the crooked brick sidewalk.)

The White Bear

i

Late autumn, day nearly gone, and weather so wild
        that bare tree limbs tore rents in the racing storm clouds,
and shreds of cloud trembled in the dank air like monstrous
        phantasmagoric rags. Rain hammered the shutters;
the roof groaned; the fire spattered and smoked.
        The sullen kettle muttered but refused to boil.
Father, mother, daughter, unspeaking, crowded into the hearth's
        fitful, flickering shadow, parents bent forward on their stools,
fingers stretched toward the guttering flame;
        the girl kneeling on the uneven bricks, poker in hand,
stirring the half-charred logs into braver action.

At each strike of metal, the red sparks leaped up
        like a swarm of maddened flies, gilding the swell of a cheek,
the bridge of a nose; casting copper over a dark sweep of hair.
        "Stop," said the mother, not snappish but tired, blank-eyed,
her complaint as rote as the kettle's; and the girl,
        crushing logs to sticks, sticks to coals, coals to cinders, barely listened,
as she barely listened to the storm beyond the door. For a moment,
        the syllable spun in the draught. Then it vanished, instantly forgotten,
like a dropped matchstick. Rain hammered the roof; the fire spat;
        a rogue twist of smoke sent the father into a spasm of coughing,
the girl dabbing soot and tears with the frayed edge of a sleeve.

Now the poker clattered onto the bricks, and the mother said,
        "Is it the shutter that's banging?" For something was beating,

beating against the cottage; or was it banging against the door?
    The windows quivered in their frames, and something
was rapping the panes—first one and then another,
    as if all the trees in the wood were begging to be let inside.
The girl rocked back on her heels, palms pressed to her hot cheeks.
    The father, still coughing, rose from his stool and the mother,
without thought, lay a hand on her daughter's shoulder,
    which trembled, not with fear but with a tense anticipation,
as a pointer trembles at the sight of her master's gun.

Yet the knocking was only the white bear, come back again.
    "May I walk in?" he asked; and meanwhile, water
roiled from the roof-edge, plashing his dense fur, which glimmered
    like pear blossoms before dawn, even amid the gale
and the rain and the darkening autumn night; meanwhile,
    his two broad paws, caked with muck, and his stout forelegs,
sullied to the elbow with leaf-mold and fir needles,
    barred the doorway, as if the bear were wary of his welcome—
or too sure of it. "Walk in," murmured the father, uneasy and shy,
    while the mother, rising from her stool, cried, "Oh, the mud!"
But already the daughter had run to fetch blankets, towels, a brush,

and the white bear had padded forward into the crescent of firelight.
    How can I explain his beauty? Even soiled with travel and storm
the bear shone in the half-dark room, glowing as a painting
    glows in the dusty corner of a church, as if once, long ago,
the canvas had swallowed all the light of the world.
    Tall as an elk, burly as an ox, he stood quietly, watchfully,
his enormous paws staining the shabby rug, his strange blue eyes
    dilating to black—though if he were beautiful,

he was also terrible. When the girl knelt before him on the rug,
　　lifting a paw onto the towel in her lap, the mud-streaked claws,
falcon-sharp and heavy as cant hooks, flashed ominously.

In haste, the parents retreated to the fire, which on the bear's entrance,
　　had roared to life. Now it burned briskly, diligent kettle
steaming on the hob, draughty room suddenly purring with heat.
　　But not with comfort. The father turned toward the flame,
his eyes carefully avoiding the bear. Less resolute, his wife
　　rattled and shifted on her stool, peeping at her silent husband,
glancing at the girl kneeling on the rain-sodden rug,
　　toweling and brushing each huge white leg; then rising to her feet
to rub the massive shoulders, the muscled back, and finally the great head,
　　pale muzzle thick as a man's arm, the tender ears rimmed with down,
and below them that terrible, unblinking, blue-black gaze.

Only after the girl had dried and brushed him, had spread a nest
　　of blankets beside the busy fire, had swept away the leaves
and fir needles and hung the dripping rug to dry, did the bear, reclining,
　　choose to speak. "Will you give me your daughter?" he asked.
On her stool, the mother looked nervously from beast to man
　　"I'm sorry," she stammered, glancing at the black-haired girl,
once again crouched on the hearth, once again beating sparks from the logs.
　　"Last time you came," whispered the woman, "she did say no."
Shifting her stool closer to her husband's, the wife touched his arm,
　　but still the man was silent, eyes fixed on the flames.
"And what does she say this time?" asked the white bear. His teeth glittered.

Swarms of sparks—violet, gold, red as witch blood—whirled in the draught.
　　Blue shadows, copper shadows fingered the girl's bowed head.

"I shall not ask again," said the bear, stretching a forepaw to the fire,
    flexing his hooked and heavy claws. "You will see me no more."
And at this warning, the girl swiftly, quietly, laid the poker on the bricks,
    and rose. Now she was taller than the reclining bear,
who lifted his white muzzle and waited, his strange eyes watchful,
    self-contained. Dangerous eyes, thought the mother.
Again she turned toward her husband, now bent forward on his stool,
    elbows on his knees, rough hands clasped. Waiting.
What will she say? thought the woman. But I know what she will say.

The white bear gazed up at the girl. The girl gazed down on the bear.
    When finally she spoke, her voice was hoarse, hurried,
almost brusque, her words pitched low. "I suppose I will go," she said.
    The father groaned and closed his eyes, and "Oh!" cried the mother,
hugging herself, suddenly cold in that overheated room.
    The bear gazed up at the girl, and his white teeth glittered.
"Fetch your things," he told her, "for we travel at moonrise."
    And while the girl was bundling her comb and her locket,
two petticoats and her winter stockings, the white bear said to her parents,
    "When your money runs low, dip the brass ladle into the well."
But the father only groaned, and the mother only hugged herself and wept.

       ii

The bear must have swallowed the storm; for now, tangled in the naked trees,
    the risen moon rocked peaceably. The rain had dwindled to a frail
feathery mist, and fragments of cloud drifted in the idle air.
    Water dripped from every needle and stalk. The brook—roaring, boastful—
charged over sedge and stone like a newborn sea. Seated on the white bear's back,
    swaying among unseen trees, down an unseen forest track,

the girl pushed back the hood of her cloak. One by one, giant raindrops, cold as fish,
        fell from the boughs and trickled slowly down her scalp.
Tightening her grip on the bear's pulsing shoulder, she stretched her free hand
        into the darkness and let her fingers brush the soft, sodden fir branches
sweeping the shadow margins of the path. All her life she had lived in this wood,

hunted its berries, trodden its tracks—but never at night, never so far, never
        at mercy of the wild. Never so alone. For since leaving the cottage,
the white bear had not spoken. First, he rested silently in the clearing,
        waiting for the girl to tuck up her skirts, to straddle his broad back,
to wedge her scanty bundle of goods beneath her cloak.
        Then he rose to his feet and padded forward into the darkness.
Behind her, framed in the bright doorway, stood her parents,
        frightened and grieving; but when she turned to call farewell,
her twisted hood smothered her words. "Good-bye," she cried, too late.
        The white bear padded forward; the swollen brook drowned her cry.
Her father and mother might never hear their child's voice again.

Tears blotched the girl's cheeks and snaked beneath her collar.
        Her feet, dangling along the bear's flanks, ached with cold.
She was wet and afraid and lost in a lonely wood, yet somehow
        she could not regret her resolve. Under her loose cloak
and crumpled skirts, the white bear's fur—rabbit-soft, blood-warm—
        rippled and flowed against her stockings . . .
but no, it was the sliver of bare thigh above her stockings
        that the fur seemed to kiss, to cradle.
Clinging to his pacing shoulder, she trailed a blind hand
        through the dripping boughs that lined the path,
licked the salt rain from her lips. She tightened her grip on the bear.

iii

Time passed. The moon, freckled and calm, had floated away
    from the clutching trees, and now her pale torch
shone down on the faint, beaten track beneath the bear's silent feet
    while the bear himself seemed to reflect the moon's light like a mirror
and cast his own watery beam into the vague and branchy wilderness.
    Presently he spoke. "Are you well?"
"I am," replied the girl on his back. But some change had come over the beast —
    a new, nervous excitement rippled from his stride;
and the terrain had shifted as well, become steeper and stonier,
    the underbrush dwindling to what might have been
clumps of lichen or moss, even heaps of pebbles.

Raindrops no longer pattered from the trees; but a dry, mild wind
    had sprung up, lifting the hem of the girl's cloak,
toying with a strand of hair. "Where are we?" she wondered aloud,
    and the white bear answered, "Nearly home."
Yet what could *home* mean? Not a cottage in the forest. Surely not a cave.
    And whose home would it be? This, the girl realized, with a clarity
that shocked her, was the question that mattered. For she had never,
    not even in anger or fantasy, been homeless. Now here she was —
foreign, adrift; and though she would not allow herself to believe
    that the bear meant to kill her, still, she had no key to any door,
and no escape, if the bear chose to bar his gates behind her.

When he reached the palace door, the white bear sank to his haunches,
    and the girl, clutching cloak and bundle, slid awkwardly to the ground,
her feet so numb that she circled and staggered like a sick horse.
    Eyes bright, breath quick, the bear rested on the silver flagstones

till she found her footing. His silence was nothing but kind;
     yet the girl, flushed with embarrassment, felt, for the first time,
a heartsick wave rise in her throat. "Oh," she cried,
     "I am so thirsty!" And indeed her throat was dry, her tongue parched,
her lips sore and split, though she had not noticed them before—
     and though she wished, instantly, that she had not complained
so babyishly, or stumbled so clumsily, or worn such thick boots.

For even as she entered the hall, this cottage girl knew
     she was at odds with the bear's palace. She might learn
to love it or fear it, but she would never roam its galleries, its lavish
     forgotten bedrooms, its roaring kitchens, its secret courtyards,
with a native's homely, ignorant abandon. Always
     she and the house would be divided. At first, she might rattle
among its stairs and winding corridors like a lentil in a sieve,
     perch on brocade with a thief's false valor.
After a dozen years, she might gain greed, custom, or disguise.
     But the language of the house—its echoes, creaks, and sighs:
that was a tongue she would never learn to speak.

Here she stood, however:
     inside a palace that was more than half mountain,
with great vaulted ceilings of granite; with winding stairways
     coiling down into the earth and up into the misty peak;
glowing with the glare of an enormous roaring fire.
     The white bear threw himself, with pleasure and abandonment,
onto a crimson carpet, stretching his paws to the flames;
     and after a few moments, the girl allowed herself to rest
on the edge of a satin ottoman. She folded her trembling hands
     over the bundle in her lap. The grandness of the room
oppressed her, and, not for the first time, she was afraid of the bear.

He seemed, at once, too glad in his surroundings
    and too indifferent to them. But what she feared,
the girl was quick to admit, for she strove to be honest with herself,
    was that the bear did not care about her fear.
She had believed, during their long journey, and especially
    at each secret, delicious touch of fur and skin,
that now and for always the white bear would understand her heart.
    But though all women make the same mistake about their lovers,
the truth is ever a shock, ever a terror.
    We convince ourselves that love will banish our loneliness.
So why, asked the girl, do I feel so alone?

        iv

It is fortunate, for all the world, that dinner assuages
    a multitude of griefs. Just as the girl felt
with a full heart that she would never be joyful again,
    a table appeared before her—one laden with scarlet linen
and white china; with spoons rubbed bright as new pennies;
    with crystal glasses and flasks; and on the plates curled
little fish fried in crumbs, alongside slivers of orange,
    and new-made butter, and potatoes split and steaming
in their jackets, and beside them a bowl of wild greens and a hot rye loaf.
    Now the white bear rose from his bed on the hearth,
and, suddenly famished, the girl also stood, dropping her bundle,

ruefully rubbing her dusty hands on her muddy skirt,
    except that, when she looked down,
the skirt was a silken gown, clean and blue as a spring sky
    and on her finger was a ring with a blue stone.

She smiled at the white bear, and the bear said,
    "Perhaps you would lift my plate to the floor."
So the girl set a plate of fish and potatoes before the bear,
    and then she sat herself down and ate.
And once the wonderful dinner was finished, a silver cake appeared.
    So the girl cut a slice for the bear and one for herself
and then, holding her slice in her hand, knelt beside him on the hearth.

Almost, now, she felt at home. The white bear licked first one paw,
    then the other. The girl brushed the crumbs from her blue dress
and said shyly, "I forgot I was hungry."
    The bear paused in his licking and turned to look at her.
As her eyes met that strange, unblinking gaze, the girl shivered;
    but this time she knew she was neither cold nor afraid.
Or perhaps she was afraid, but with a species of fear
    she did not recognize as fear. For his gaze was a stream of light,
devouring and stern, yet also (and this was the marvel) a plea.
    "And are you tired?" asked the bear softly.
The girl looked down at her hands, then into his eyes. "I am," she said.

    v

She has forgotten the room, forgotten the firelight, forgotten
    the cool ironed sham beneath her cheek,
forgotten the shadows under the bed, forgotten the wind at the window,
    the stars burning, an owl snatching a wayward rabbit,
the rabbit's shriek; she has forgotten her mother, her father,
    her cottage under moonlight; forgotten the rain,
forgotten the brook that wept like a river.
    Only now only now only now.

For dreaming and the act of love are mirrors;
　　and tonight the girl knows also; but where is her breath,
where is the tender shivering flesh below the ridge of her shoulder?

Where? For she has lost herself, she has lost the white bear,
　　who is not a bear, but what has he become?
What has she become? Both have cast off their skins, both
　　grown larger than giants, and each new and solitary cell
undergoes its ruthless joy. Who is the bear, who the woman;
　　who the air, who the fire; who the knife,
who the wound? How terrible they are;
　　how near to hate and dreaming is love,
its fury of nail and claw; and how time
　　narrows and slows, till now there is only
yes and no and yes.

　　　　vi

But such interludes are finite.
　　Though at night the beast cast off the form of a bear,
he reappeared as a beast in the morning,
　　day after day, week after week,
and meanwhile winter came to the mountain palace.
　　The fires roared high and the snow fell,
and when the girl breathed on the frosted mullions
　　and rubbed away her breath, she saw only white stones
against white sky. Inside the palace she possessed all
　　that an intelligent young woman is prone to desire —
galleries and libraries, hothouses and kitchens,

and a fierce and tireless lover. Yet the palace oppressed her,
    as it had oppressed her from the first.
Perhaps, she thought, as she idled in the window seat,
    scratching small patterns on the frost panes,
I am tired of having everything chosen for me.
    Or perhaps I am merely a discontented woman.
And she thought of the tales she had read,
    of greedy sisters and unhappy queens
and meek, obedient goose-girls; and she sighed
    and leaned her cheek against the cold glass,
and let the heavy book on her lap slip to the floor.

That evening, as she knelt before the fire,
    tilting the dregs of dark wine back and forth,
back and forth in her glass, she said to the white bear
    who lay stretched beside her,
"I wonder what my mother and father are doing now."
    The white bear rolled over and lifted his head.
"What do you want?" he asked.
    The girl tilted her wineglass back and forth,
and the dregs flashed and darkened,
    flashed and darkened.
"Oh," she said, and paused. And then:

"My hours in this palace trickle away so slowly.
    Perhaps I am dull; perhaps winter
is lonely. But at home, they needed me —
    to carry firewood, to cook breakfast, to wash clothes."
Quietly the bear replied, "This is your home, and I need you."
    Though his words were gentle, his pale eyes

sharpened. The girl dropped her gaze.

He was wrong: his home was not her home.
She knew she would always be a stranger in his vast, stony palace.

Nonetheless, she loved him, she loved him terribly;
and she needed him to love her.

This the bear understood. And after their months together,
the white bear was learning (or beginning to learn)
that he, too, must bend. "Dear one," he said,
and his voice was calm,
"I will send you to visit your parents,
but you must make me a promise,
and you must keep your word."

The girl turned toward him and laid a hand
on his broad shoulder. Now she wrapped both arms
around him and pressed her nose into his warm neck.
The bear repeated, more softly yet, "You *must* keep your word."

The girl said quickly, her tumbled words muffled
against the bear's heavy fur, "I will keep my word, of course."
Only then did she remember that she did not know
what she was promising.
She raised her head. "But why?" she said. "What must I do?"

"It is what you must not do that matters," replied the bear.
"You must not allow your mother to lead you away from your father
and speak of me. You must not,
or both you and I will suffer." Cupping her two hands
around the white bear's muzzle, the girl bent
to kiss its bridge. "That will not happen," she said.

vii

And in less than a moment
 she stood before her parents' forest cottage
at winter's bare end. All around her
 heaved boot-riven mud. The snow, half-melted,
was soiled with blackened leaves and gnawed pinecones;
 chips and sawdust littered the dooryard. And yet
smoke threaded so joyously from the chimney; a chickadee
 whistled his high-low spring song; sunlight
fingered the barren trees; and a small, soft wind tugged at her cloak.
 The very window-glass seemed to blink at her with pleasure.
The girl was so swiftly, so deeply happy that she hesitated to knock.

But she took a breath and, tears prickling her eyes, tapped at the door.
 Inside, a thump and a flurry: her mother
dropping the rolling pin and now scraping flour paste
 from her hands, and now the thud of her clogs
as she bustled to the door, and now
 such crying and kissing and embracing;
and "oh, how beautiful she is, my lost child;
 how brightly her dress gleams under the velvet cloak;
how the little blue ring sparkles on her finger!"
 Now the father stamps his boots at the back door;
his daughter flies into his arms, spilling his bucket of twigs,

nearly cracking his head on the doorframe: more cries and kissing,
 and then, at long last, three heads round the kitchen table,
cups in hand, kettle steaming on the hob; and the mother saying,
 "Tell us everything, my love."

So the girl set down her teacup and retold the tale of her travels —
      her long ride on the white bear's back, her arrival at the palace
in the mountain, the kindness of the bear, the wonderful dinners
      and kitchens and libraries of her new home.
Her father listened in wide-eyed wonder, and when he brought himself
      to question his daughter, he spoke like the craftsman he was.
So she detailed the marble floors, the oaken shelves, the smooth slate counters.

But her mother had other curiosities. "My love," she said,
      clasping her daughter's hand between her own,
"tell us about your husband. Is he kind to you?"
      At mention of the white bear, the girl found herself
longing to speak of him. But she remembered his warning
      and turned the conversation into other routes —
speaking of the fine thick carpet on the cottage floor
      and the silver tankards twinkling on the shelf;
for the bear had been as good as his word. Whenever
      the parents were in need, they dipped the brass ladle
into the well and brought forth a dipper full of coins.

And since they were not extravagant, they lived snugly enough,
      lamenting their daughter but day by day regaining
a certain sweet content in themselves, as parents must do.
      Indeed, as the weeks of her visit passed,
the girl began to see herself as an imposition to their comfort —
      not that her parents promoted this view;
but three stools crowded the hearth,
      the coat pegs no longer held space for her cloak,
and the apple tart divided awkwardly for three.
      Once three had been the most natural of numbers.
Could she blame them for making the best of two,

especially now that she had become half of two herself?
    For oh, how she missed the white bear!
Each night, as she lay wrapped in her blanket by the fire,
    her thoughts returned to the palace fireside,
to the bear's great paws curling on the flagstones,
    to the heat of his breath on her breast;
and she turned and tossed, trapped in the peculiar despair
    of unsubstantiated desire, angry at her ingratitude —
to her lover, whom she had willingly deserted;
    to her parents, who fussed and fidgeted from morning till night.
If only she could speak of the bear to someone, anyone!

The girl took to wandering away of an afternoon, far down the forest track,
    merely for the chance to lie among the broken remnants
of last year's bracken ferns and whisper the bear's name. Her parents,
    puzzled and sad, watched her disappear into the woods;
yet they were not more puzzled than their daughter, nor more sad.
    She did not think to ponder, "So what, after all, does home mean?"
as she lay in her damp cot and watched the finches, garbed in their winter drab,
    flicker from bough to bough; but the question nonetheless
dangled before her in the listless air; and when finally she sat up, stiff with cold,
    and gathered strength for her mother's too-cheerful greeting,
her father's anxious frown, she had advanced not a step toward contentment.

    viii

And it was in this low state that she made her error.
    The day had opened in wet fog, and as the morning passed,
rain began to fall steadily. With no hope of escape into the forest,
    the girl sat moodily at the table sorting sprouted onions for the pig —

a simple-enough task in itself yet wretchedly tedious
    if one is the lovesick queen of an enchanted palace.
Her mother sat on a stool by the fire, mending a shirt; but her father,
    braving the rain, had walked into the village, his pocket
stuffed with coins from the well, the vision of a little mare filling his thoughts.
    Surely a little mare would cheer his daughter, give her a new care.
Somehow he never allowed himself to consider that she might leave again.

Nor, it seems, had his wife. Early that morning, still abed,
    he had broached the idea, and she, all smiles, had eagerly agreed.
"The blacksmith has a horse he would sell—a beautiful mare,
    spotted, with a long black tail. Walk down to the forge, my dear;
offer him a good price; and meanwhile, I will speak to our daughter alone.
    Perhaps I may discover what the bear has done to create such misery."
The plan was kind, and the woman meant well indeed.
    But it may be that every loving parent has made a similar mistake.
For we have been so long trained to defend our children's joy
    that we are too liable to hate the pains of that joy
and distrust the thieving lover who has coaxed them forth.

So as the daughter sorted onions, the mother spoke to her gently
    but with a mother's expectation of obedience.
"You must tell me, now, about the white bear. You are so unhappy,
    yet how can I help you if I know nothing?"
Though a mother's aid was no use in this matter, this was a fact
    that neither mother nor daughter recognized.
And after all, the girl was so very tired of silence.
    She would say a few words, no more than a few,
just to satisfy her mother's curiosity. There could be no harm.
    Surely the bear knew how much she loved him; surely
he had never meant her to relinquish all mention of his name.

The girl sighed, straightened her shoulders, shook the papery fragments
    of onionskin from her skirts. Then she turned toward her mother
and, folding her dusty hands in her lap, opened her mouth to speak.
    But as soon as the word *bear* fell from her lips,
the whole tale of their love burst forth. Weeping, she told her mother
    that every night the bear came to her bed and that perhaps,
in truth, he was not a bear—she wasn't sure, she couldn't explain,
    he might have been a man, yet she never saw him in the darkness;
oh, but he was kind, very kind, and she loved him dearly;
    nothing was wrong, only she was lonely and out of sorts;
the bear had never hurt her, never really hurt her. He was very kind.

The mother listened to this tale of woe with a kind of open-eyed horror
    melding embarrassment with fear. But it was also
(though this she only vaguely admitted to herself) tinged with envy.
    A faithful husband is a lifetime's comfort, but who among us
grows immune to dreams of a mysterious ardent lover?
    And yet her child, her child, in the grip of such confusion!
"My darling," cried the mother, rising so violently from her seat
    that her basket of sewing toppled, and thimble and spools
clattered onto the floor and rolled away, forgotten, into the corners.
    "What if your husband is a troll?"
"Oh, mother," wept the girl, "you're wrong. It can't be true."

Yet once the words had been spoken, she could not forget them,
    especially after her father returned from the village
leading the spotted mare. Stroking the mare's soft nose,
    the girl discovered, tied to the bridle, a long red ribbon;
and on it, printed in gold, these instructions:
    "Ride into the forest, and I will meet you."

"What shall I do?" she cried; but already, as her stricken parents
    begged her to stay, she had snatched up her cloak,
flung it over her shoulders, and mounted the dancing mare,
    who galloped headlong into the fog and vanished
before the father could gather strength or wits to hold her.

ix

There was no sign of the white bear. Nonetheless,
    the little mare trotted briskly along the path,
her pace so confident and surefooted that the girl
    soon dropped the reins and let them lie untended in her lap.
At first she had peered ahead anxiously into the fog,
    quick to spy any glimmer of white among the trees;
but as the hours passed and no bear appeared,
    she found her attention wavering, her eyes beginning to close;
felt herself falling forward, cheek pillowed against the mare's
    sweet-scented mane, as the horse, unchecked, trotted on
and the scent, rising and falling like breath, became a dream.

And this is what she dreamed —
    a door opening into a dark room,
one she had never seen before, a room cavernous with shadows
    yet here was the little bed she had slept in last night
before her parents' fire. Why was it here, in this strange room,
    and who was sleeping in it? A guttering stub of candle
appeared in her hand; she lifted it high over the bed;
    and there lay a man, fair as snow,

fast asleep beneath a white bearskin. She leaned over him,
    thinking she must faint if she did not
brush her lips against his bare shoulder;

but as she bent over him, three drops of wax fell,
    searing three scars like tears into his pale skin.
Starting up suddenly from sleep, he cried out,
    "What have you done? What have you done?"
"Oh, oh," sobbed the girl, for she knew, now, who he was.
    "You have spoken to your mother," he replied, and the three scars
pulsed like starlight in the black room. "Let our misery begin."
    At these words, the girl wailed and wept; she threw herself into his arms,
she kissed his wrists, his hands, begging for mercy . . .
    But at this moment she awoke and found herself clutching
the mare's black mane and the mare galloping full tilt into the darkness.

"Stop!" shrieked the girl.
    Instantly the mare halted, with such force that the girl
tumbled forward into the ferns. There she sat, dizzy and breathless,
    as the mare idly nibbled a dry leaf.
"Where are you running to, little mare?" stammered the girl,
    her voice choking in her throat;
for she knew now that the horse was no common village hack.
    Perhaps, like her own white bear, the mare could speak;
perhaps she *was* the bear, in new form;
    and at this thought, the girl leaped to her feet
and put her two arms round the horse's slender neck.

"Dear mare," she asked, "who are you?"
    The mare only snorted and flicked her ears.

As she did so, an acorn fell into the girl's lap,
    then split cleanly at the cap, as acorns will;
and inside the cap was printed the word *East* in fine gold script,
    but around the nut marched the word *West* in silver capitals.
"What does it mean?" wailed the girl, flinging cap and nut
    into the bracken. "I don't believe it means anything at all."
The white bear, hidden in the bracken and watching her,
    may have thought twice about his choice of wife —
this angry, tear-stained, red-faced girl, her cloak checkered with leaf-mold,

shouting fruitlessly at the spotted mare,
    though, in truth, the mare seemed indifferent to the clamor,
merely lifting a hind hoof to scratch the back of a front knee.
    The girl hid her face in her hands, tried to breathe deeply,
tried to think. East, west; east, west . . . with such instructions,
    she might just as well dig her own barrow,
here, under these twigs, this bracken; leave the mare to find her way home,
    or wherever it was she might be heading.
And at this thought, the girl lifted her face from her hands.
    "Where were you going? Who were you running to?" she asked.
In response, the mare whinnied and pranced and flung her head,

from which actions the girl took a bit of comfort —
    not happiness, to be sure, nor even confidence;
more as if the cloud on her heart had shifted its shape.
    At least the horse claimed to know which road to travel.
Wearily, she clambered to her feet; wearily, she remounted.
    "Go where you are going," she said,
and instantly the mare darted forward into the forest,
    the girl bobbing listlessly on her back.

Tears welled from her swollen eyes and spilled down her blotchy cheeks.
    She wiped her nose on the edge of her cloak.
What have I become? wondered the girl, but only briefly.

For she had entered that strange realm of selfishness
    that arises only in moments of great misery,
when despair becomes a kind of spell,
    and sorrow creates its own walled castle.
Everything outside the girl seemed vaporous and indistinct.
    No longer did she scan the forest for sight of the white bear.
He would not come. No one would come.
    Clinging to the back of this jogging beast,
she would ride through the night, and then through another night.
    One by one, the stars would flare and fade and flicker out,
and the moon would turn her face to the wall.

        x

Here is where my tale becomes difficult to write,
    where it swells and dissipates and trails away to mist.
For not only do my characters refuse to behave admirably;
    they also—and this is the crux—
they refuse to behave with resolve.
    The bear, of course, was angry with his wife;
and for a time his anger overtopped his loneliness.
    He lay hidden in the brush as she tumbled into the ferns.
He watched her fling the acorn message into the dark,
    and he felt a certain satisfaction at sight of her harridan misery.
But don't think that the white bear was, at heart, a cruel husband.

Words came hard to him. He was, after all, more beast than man;
    and though he loved his wife, and longed for her return,
her angers and fears were nothing to his own.
    In his eyes, they were petty, staged for display,
overrun with tears and fine speeches, while his own —
    ah, his animal flame ran wordless and deep, like molten stone.
Or so he believed. The bear's wife, who loved him fiercely,
    might have chosen "chill" instead of "flame,"
"claw" instead of "stone," "prideful" instead of "deep."
    Who, if not a wife, sees a man more clearly than he sees himself?
Or so she believes.

The little mare, insouciant, trotted away into the dark.
    The bear, hidden and silent among the bracken,
lay glowering at the girl on the horse's back.
    The girl rubbed a knuckle into her swollen eyes
and, with her other hand, tightened her grip on the horse.
    She felt obliged, suddenly, to make a decision,
any decision, one would be as good as the next,
    she was exhausted by love, by anger,
she hated love, she would go home to her parents
    and tell them nothing, she would lie, day and night,
tearless on her bed. The white bear had betrayed her,

or she had betrayed him, and there was no use
    in trying to recover what they had lost.
"East, west," she said to the horse.
    And then suddenly she said, "Go north."
At those words, the mare turned suddenly
    and plunged into the thicket.

The tree branches leaned forward, scratching and plucking at the girl,
    who screamed, covering her head with her arms
as the mare swerved among the terrible trees.
    And the white bear, who lay hidden among the bracken
and brush to the south of the path, silently got to his feet.

For a moment he stood motionless,
    shimmering like the moon on this moonless night.
Then he turned his back to the trail, and he padded away.

Cinderella Story

Given these twenty-below-zero nights —
gale winds straight from the Siberian plains of hell,
and every tormented tree in the forest groaning its misery —
this mourning dove should be dead.

Yet here she crouches, hogging the feeder tray,
pebble-eyed and jaunty despite the ice cube
that, for two arctic days, has encased her pink left foot
like an elegant cement overshoe.

Persistent chickadees flutter and dip,
yearning to snatch a perch. The dove,
eight times their size and oblivious to complaint,
just keeps gobbling. In woodpecker fashion,

she's clamped her broad tail over the tray edge
for balance, yet all the while her icebound foot,
a rosy block of sparkles, dangles in the knife-edge breeze.
Among these busy airborne birdlets,

her shackle swings like a locket packed with lead shot.
Even so, I'm tempted to circle
optimism on the metaphysical scorecard.
After all, the bird's not dead, not even almost dead,

though no doubt her frostbitten foot
will rot and fall off, and she'll be forced to endure
a blackened stump for the balance of her brief days —
that is, if a fox or my own cheerful dog doesn't

hunt her down at twilight and break her neck.
Yesterday my son was clutching me in panic:
"What can we do? What can we do?"
But today he forgets to notice her.

The dove has become ordinary window dressing.
She gobbles seed; she snaps her beak at finches;
she flaps heavily into the snow-stiffened boughs.
Her feathers gleam and her beady eye glitters.

From where we stand—
here: in our kitchen, our own snug invention—
any happy can look like an ending.

The Years

Dreamy as Tarzan, the years murmur
their old tune as we stride away from them

into our spotlit lives. Like fathers, they armor
    themselves against loss, hawking phlegm

    into coffee cans, scratching their scaly pates,
though a Nehi odor lingers in their cough,

faint as sour cream. Behind their rusty agate
    stare slides a slow-rolling map of sloughed-

    off days along the river. Scabby grapevines
grip the porch rails, courting light. A peahen

chitters in the weeds, and on the clothesline
    the half-yellowed shirts of sweating men

sag like idle hands. The years hum our quavered names.
We clench our fists: panicked, ruthless, dumb, ashamed.

V

Hell, everyone keeps a light on in the front hall until they go to bed.

—Eugene O'Neill, *Long Day's Journey into Night*

Accident Report

You know how it is:
tires devouring the coiled road,
one hand on the wheel, bending left,
bending right, slick as a seal; one of those
dawns when grains of fog spatter your windshield
like handfuls of sand, when a monstrous owl drifts

from the invisible forest with a rat writhing in his claws;
when a half-grown buck, leaf-drunk, vaults across the sopping
tarmac like a prince under enchantment; and "Whoso list to hunt,
I know where is an hind!" you cry, but silently, of course, because . . .
because you're ashamed to mouth a greater poet's borrowed trappings;
you, with no rights in the matter, mere remote control in fog, ambivalent,

wishful, and cold as well; for all the heat's in words you were afraid to sing
in earshot of these phantoms—Wyatt, Milton—floating in the vinyl shade,
ready to taunt your match-struck quavering flame. You, not man enough
to warble to an empty car; they, so long dead, still young: still flashing
their brash "So help me God, an immortality of fame." They played
their necessary cards: not only intellect and drudgery and grief,

wordy sleight-of-hand and rage and loving, probing curiosity,
but plain obnoxious gall. A poem, a stiletto in the back.
And you, alone and lonely, in your blundering car,
afraid of some fool prince with the temerity
to leap into your high-beam's timid dark.
As if that murky light could be his star.

Bargain Shopper

I miss you, Jilline, though stuck in this frozen so-called spring
I don't picture you regretting my grim haunts; you, the girl
Who adored high summer, sporting your cheap slinky cling-
Tight blouses, those cat-eye shades propped in your dyed curls,
Your pink-flowered skirts, and a pair of flapping tacky lamé slides
On your big sore feet. Your beau-idée of taste was a dollar sale
At Marshall's, the two of us name-dropping Ruskin and Gide,
Stage-whispering, "There's your boyfriend," across the gaudy aisles
At first sight of every funny-looker we met: those goat-
Faced circus clowns, those clad-entirely-in-blue albinos—
What freaks wandered this earth! . . . and you, decked out
Like a discount drag queen, lovingly deriding my beige vinyl
     Sandals half-mended with bread ties. Only your puff of frail hair
     Mentioned you were dying. The freaks pretended not to stare.

The Fate of Captain Fetterman's Command

1866

At first light we saw our enemies
on the bluff
silver flashing in their hair

a glory of sun as they rode away laden
with tunics saddles boots arrows
still piercing the cracked boots

piercing our silent comrades
and just visible in the dawn
we saw wolves and coyotes

skulking along the verge
crows buzzards eagles circling
the sun-spattered meadow

but not one white body was disturbed
for we hear that salt permeates
the whole system of our race

which protects us from the wild
to some degree but it was strange
that nothing had eaten the horses either

except for flies which swarmed in thick
like the stench
all day we waited

till the doctor finished his report then
they told us to pack our friends
into the ammunition wagons

this was our job they said to retch
to stumble into the field to grasp
at wrists at ankles dissolving to pulp

under our grip to vomit to weep
to stare at masks pounded bloody with stones
bloated crawling with flies who were they

this was our job but we could not sort
cavalry from infantry all stripped
naked slashed skulls crushed

with war clubs ears noses legs
hacked off and some had
crosses cut on their breasts

faces to the sky
we walked on their hearts
but did not know it in the high grass

Clockwork

And on her mind is all the waste
    and the waiting, and the pain
        of wanting someone to listen
to the pain she can't talk about, like how her lover
    is a drunk, and how she is afraid
        of time and of her mind
circling its mud-wrenched, idiot track.
    And meanwhile a neighbor expires
        in a strange bed, little birds
flutter in the bony lilacs,
    her lover slides another blank-faced bottle
        under the torn seat of his pickup.
Wind blunders among the empty branches,
    raking their frail tips against a livid sky.
        Another hour lost, she thinks, but hours later,
in the medicated dark, her mind
    and what's on her mind keep ticking, ticking,
        stupidly ticking on.

Notes from a Traffic Jam

Roadmaster truck creaking up from its netherworld,
swaying past the fizzing lights of a diner,
then sliding like a boxy snake into the unremembered night —

Window glimpse of optimists on a couch,
bending forward in eager profile to toast Fortune
with a pair of giant paper cups —

Oh, sometimes I fear I've lost the will to imagine
this comedy, this ugly beauty, this moving-picture world.
On and on it runs, trundling out the bumpkin tale of our species

yet wanting nothing from me: neither eye nor heart,
nor sneer, nor timid idle word. I bide my time in this car
like a beetle trapped on a floating weed, biting my nails,

squinting into the disembodied glare of your lanterns,
but you, you, you are a million dream-years away —
You, closing your India-print curtains against the dark;

you, shifting your haunches, humming your tune.
When I remember to hate myself,
I hate myself for not loving you enough —

You, who never lay a thought upon me.

Epilogue

The Chariot

Hooves pounding on bronze; a long, wild, whinnying chorus,
and the horses were airborne, eight enormous wings
beating, swishing, beating. Without warning, wind
crammed a fist into Phaeton's mouth, jabbed knives
into his nose, his ears. Legs churning, wings flailing,
the steeds cut through cloud, through hissing vapors
that melted under their fiery breath. The driver, careening
from side to side in the clattering chariot, clung to the reins.

His father's instructions flashed through his mind:
"Hold back the horses." Phaeton dragged at the reins,
but his wrists were unsteady, his weight was light;
he was a fly compared to the god; and the giddy horses,
unchecked by any master, lunged and galloped.
Traces tangled with reins, the yoke twisted,
a sharp hoof sliced a flank, a spray of bloody foam
whipped Phaeton's parched eyes.

In a panic, the child threw the whole weight of his rigid body

against the reins, jerking them left, then right,

trying to find the middle road, to guide the plunging horses

into their familiar wheel tracks. But he had no clear idea

of where the road might lie. Beyond the horses' flaming breath,

he glimpsed cloud and rippled patches of sky, of Dawn

hastily folding her lustrous cloak, and now, to his horror,

bright-zoned Orion leaping away from the hurtling chariot.

Phaeton no longer knew if he gripped the reins.

Terrified of the reeling heavens, of the Crab scuttling crazily

toward the Archer, of the wakened Bear, snarling, furious,

he looked down, far down, at puddle lakes, groves of grass blades,

tine-scratched fields no bigger than eggs.

The heat . . . this unrelenting glare . . .

His fiery crown oppressed him, his knees gave way:

Oh, why had he wished for such a father?

Now his birth seemed worse than nothing.

If only he had been the son of Vulcan,

contentedly chipping nymphs from stone,

mapping Ocean with a chisel, patiently mopping

a mild sweat from his uncrowned brow.

If only that happy boy chasing goats

away from his mother's grapevine

had never stared into the sky and desired the Sun.

Dazzled, stricken, Phaeton cowered against the chariot floor.

The reins slipped from his fingers and slid away,

falling loosely over the horses' backs. Now wholly free,

they bolted ahead, then veered to the side, then galloped forward again,

the chariot crashing and buckling in their wake.

High, higher, they raced into the scattering stars and then plunged

wildly toward Earth, and whatever they touched, they destroyed.

Clouds scorched and withered; great Parnassus burst into flame,

and on the mountaintops, snow dissolved to rivers of steam.

In a moment entire forests burned like tinder.

A house, a loom, a woman. Gone.

Cities vanished in walls of fire; even Ocean gaped.

Trapped in a hot waste of sand, the sea nymphs screamed;

Neptune, lifting his trident to heaven, bellowed for aid,

the winds were choked with ash; Earth burned, burned;

and on Olympus Zeus stood watching, in silence.

Notes & Acknowledgments

In the book's opening epigraph, I reprint William Shakespeare's sonnet 76 (ca. 1609) as it appears in *The Riverside Shakespeare*, ed. G. Blakemore Evans (Boston: Houghton Mifflin, 1974), 1763, although I've deleted the scholarly brackets in line 7.

The poems that form the prologue and the epilogue owe a structural debt to Ovid, "The Story of Phaeton," in *Metamorphoses* (ca. A.D. 1), trans. Rolphe Humphries (Bloomington: Indiana University Press, 1955), 28–40.

The section epigraphs are from Iris Murdoch's *The Black Prince* (New York: Viking, 1973), 44; George Eliot's *Felix Holt, the Radical* (1866; reprint, Harmondsworth, Middlesex, U.K.: Penguin, 1972), 117; Dorothy L. Sayers's *Busman's Honeymoon* (1937; reprint, New York: Avon, 1968), 9; William Shakespeare's *King Lear* (ca. 1605), in *The Riverside Shakespeare*, 1270; and Eugene O'Neill's *Long Day's Journey into Night* (New Haven, Conn.: Yale University Press, 1956), 126.

"Blue in Green" refers to a track on the Miles Davis album *Kind of Blue* (New York: Columbia Records, 17 August 1959). The title of "No Day Is Safe from News of You" quotes from Sylvia Plath's "The Rival," in *Ariel* (Boston: Harper & Row, 1961), 48. The quotation in "Shouting at

Shakespeare" is from William Shakespeare's sonnet 85 (ca. 1609), in *The Riverside Shakespeare*, 1764. "Mrs. Dickinson Waits in the Car" quotes from Emily Dickinson's letter to Thomas Wentworth Higginson, 25 April 1862, collected in the Dickinson Electronic Archives; the last stanza of the poem quotes from Percy Bysshe Shelley's "A Defence of Poetry," in *The Percy Reprints*, no. 3, ed. H. F. B. Brett-Smith (Boston: Houghton Mifflin, 1921), 53, and Joe Bolton's "The Circumstances," in *The Last Nostalgia: Poems 1982–1990*, ed. Donald Justice (Fayetteville: University of Arkansas Press, 1999), 125. "The White Bear" was triggered by the Scandinavian fairy tale "East of the Sun and West of the Moon," collected in *The Blue Fairy Book*, ed. Andrew Lang (1889; reprint, Mineola, N.Y.: Dover), 19–29. "The Years" borrows its title from Virginia Woolf's eponymous novel (1937; reprint, New York: Harcourt, 1939) and opens with a phrase from Richard Ford's *The Sportswriter* (New York: Random House, 1986), 207. "Accident Report" quotes from Thomas Wyatt's "Whoso list to hunt" (ca. 1557) as it appears in *The Making of a Sonnet: A Norton Anthology*, ed. Edward Hirsch and Eavan Boland (New York: Norton, 2008), 79; and from John Milton's letter to Charles Diodati, 23 November 1637, excerpted in Barbara Lewalski, *The Life of John Milton* (Oxford: Blackwell, 2000), 33. "The Fate of Captain Fetterman's Command" was influenced by eyewitness accounts quoted in Evan S. Connell, *Son of the Morning Star: Custer and the Little Bighorn* (New York: North Point, 1984), 128–32.

I am grateful to the editors of the following journals for publishing my poems, sometimes in different formats or under different titles:

Aurorean: "Cover Song," "Dog in Winter"
Best Poems: "The Chariot," "Driving Lesson"
Green Mountains Review: excerpts from "The White Bear"
Guernica: "Son-in-Law"
LocusPoint: "Accident Report," "Cinderella Story," "Shouting at

Shakespeare," "Valentine's Day," "The Years"

New Walk: "Ugly Town"

Poetry Salzburg Review: "No Day Is Safe from News of You"

roger: "Home"

Sewanee Review: "The Fate of Captain Fetterman's Command"

Solstice: "Astrolabe," "Spring on the Ripley Road"

Sou'wester: "Clockwork"

Unrorean: "Letter to Will"

U.S. 1 Worksheets: "Bargain Shopper"

"After Twenty Years" appeared in *You Must Remember This: Poems about Aging and Memory*, ed. Gordon Lang and Barbara Bald (Poetry Society of New Hampshire, 2013). "Blue" and "Mrs. Dickinson Waits in the Car" appeared in *Gathered: Contemporary Quaker Poets*, ed. Nick McRae (Sundress, 2013).

I also thank Nate Fisher, who read early versions of several of these poems; Will Agranoff, Baron Wormser, and Annaliese Jakimides, who generously commented on the manuscript; and Stuart Kestenbaum, director of Haystack Mountain School of Crafts, who invited me to the school's 2010 New Works faculty retreat, where I first discovered that I'd written this book.

CavanKerry's Mission

CavanKerry Press is a not-for-profit literary press dedicated to art and community. From its inception in 2000, its vision has been to present, through poetry and prose, *Lives Brought to Life* and to create programs that bring CavanKerry books and writers to diverse audiences.

Other Books in the Notable Voices Series